CROWNED HEART SERIES — BOOK THREE

Corinne True

Written by Melanie Lotfali

Illustrated by Katayoun Mottahedin

The Crowned Heart Series – Corinne True

Text © Copyright Melanie Lotfali
Illustrations © Copyright Katayoun Mottahedin
Original book design by Monib Mahdavi

First Edition 2008
Second Edition 2016
All Rights Reserved

Licensed under a Creative Commons
Attribution-NonCommercial-ShareAlike 4.0
International License

www.melanielotfali.com

hardcover ISBN 978-0-9946018-2-7
softcover ISBN 978-0-9945926-9-9

How many queens of the world have laid down their heads on a pillow of dust and disappeared… Not so the handmaids who ministered at the Threshold of God; these have shone forth like glittering stars in the skies of ancient glory, shedding their splendors across all the reaches of time.

'Abdu'l-Bahá

There are queens who wear crowns on their heads. Their crowns are made of earthly things like gold and diamonds and rubies.

And there are queens who wear crowns in their hearts. Their crowns are made of heavenly things, like love and courage and humility. This is the story about one of those queens.
Her name is Corinne True.

Corinne True had eight children. She loved them all very much. Four of her children went early to the Abha Kingdom. Corinne True was very sad. 'Abdu'l-Bahá told her the children were with Bahá'u'lláh. He said they were happy. Corinne True developed strength and courage.

'Abdu'l-Bahá gave Mother True a big job to do. He wanted her to help build a Bahá'í Temple in North America.

Mother True worked very hard. She wrote lots of letters. She organised lots of meetings.

She helped gather the money to pay for the temple. She also helped find a good place to build it. And she prayed!

'Abdu'l-Bahá visited the place where the temple was going to be built. He thought it was a wonderful place. 'Abdu'l-Bahá gave the Bahá'ís a special prayer to say for the temple. Corinne True must have said that prayer a lot!

It took a long time to build the temple. When it was finished Mother True was very old and also very happy.

Mother True lived for ninety-nine years. Each year she added heavenly gems to the crown in her heart. The gem of determination shines especially bright in her heart's crown.

Hand of the Cause of God
Corinne True

REFERENCES

The stories and facts contained in this book are from:
 Harper, Barron. "*Lights of Fortitude*". August, 1997.
 George Ronald, Oxford, Great Britain.

Melanie Lotfali

Melanie Lotfali PhD is a graduate of the Australian College of Journalism in Professional Writing for Children. She is the author of the Fellowship Farm series, Unity in Diversity series, and Crowned Heart series.

She currently lives in Townsville, Australia, with her family.

Katayoun Mottahedin

Katayoun Mottahedin has a Post Graduate Diploma of Education from Monash University, Bachelor of Graphic Design from Swinburne University of Technology and Diploma of Arts and Design from Chisholm Institute. Her art has been utilised in magazines, books, greeting cards, stationary and other publications.

She currently lives in Melbourne, Australia.

www.ingramcontent.com/pod-product-compliance
Lightning Source LLC
Chambersburg PA
CBHW042229010526
44113CB00046B/2946